D1506455

The
Mafia Manager

The Mafia Manager

A Guide to the Corporate Machiavelli

St. Martin's Griffin ⋈ New York

A THOMAS DUNNE BOOK.
An imprint of St. Martin's Press.

THE MAFIA MANAGER. Copyright © 1991, 1996 by Curtis L. Johnson.
All rights reserved. Printed in the United States of America.
For information, address St. Martin's Press, 175 Fifth Avenue,
New York, N.Y. 10010.

Design by Songhee Kim

Library of Congress Cataloging-in-Publication Data

V.
     The Mafia manager / by "V".
        p.   cm.
     "A Thomas Dunne book."
     ISBN 978-0-312-15574-2
     1. Management.   2. Personnel management.   I. Title.
HD31.V25   1996
658—dc20   95-41004
                                                        CIP

D 30 29 28

For Rocky, Spike, and Charlie

You can get a lot more done with a kind word and a gun than with a kind word alone.

—*Al Capone*

Contents

Part III — The Rest of It

Introduction

No matter what their occupation—and no matter if self-employed or corporate climber—getting ahead and staying ahead has long been a major concern of all who are not content with merely earning a living. In their eager, sometimes feverish, pursuit of a personal pot of gold (and the power and prestige that come with it), ambitious men and women have sought the knowledge of those who have achieved success before them. *The Mafia Manager* provides such knowledge, of a particular sort, for the first time.

The bedrock secret of success can be summarized as this: Find a place in the system where you manage others. To find such a place, if you start with no inherited wealth, you must be more intelligent, ambitious, and vigorous than your competition. And if you are to succeed greatly in the world's terms, you must also be lucky—and ruthless. Live with wolves, and you will learn to howl.

Once you find your place, you must be able to keep it, defend it against attack from your rivals, and improve upon it. Many will contend for your place because such places reward the holder inordinately. To hold it, you must be clearheaded—and (again) ruthless.

You will know the people to know in your world, and they will know you and trust and use you, as you use them. There is an understanding in these matters: You do favors and carry out certain assigned undertakings; you know what should be done and what cannot be, and you know what your share will be. In return for your goodwill and services, you have the backing of sponsors with even greater power. And so you work your way up. And up.

The common thread that runs through most of the great success stories in the cut-throat, complex world of business is this: A majority of those who rise to the top are adept in the art of managing others. Part of their talent as managers is perhaps innate, part perhaps acquired through experience, and part no doubt a reflection of the acute intelligence peculiar to some, but not all, of the successful.

There are books in vast profusion examining and analyzing the management techniques of successful corporation executives and business tycoons. But most of these volumes are simply recitations of theories widely held to be fact in corporate circles and by academics—part of the standard MBA curriculum. They are, that is, purveyors of the conventional wisdom—which is, as is well known to successful managers—invariably wrong. These works go on superficially at great length and serve only to entrench error.

What none of these texts has ever presented is this: the distilled wisdom of the men who have managed one of the largest, most profitable and long-lived cartels in the history of capitalism—organized crime or as it is variously called, the Mafia, La Cosa Nostra, the Syndicate, the Mob, the Outfit, and half a dozen other appellations.

The Mafia Manager gathers for the first time in one book the knowledge and precepts of the ruthless bosses whose genius at organization and management contributed far more to profitability and growth than did the brute strength and recourse to violence of the common, unsophisticated gangster—or the conventional wisdom of the legitimate CEO.

Unlike other volumes on the principles of sound management, *The Mafia Manager* cuts through the verbiage (and exceedingly dull and often pointless case histories that accompany it) to succinctly present the pragmatism and guiding philosophy of the leadership that founded and captained "The Silent Empire" through its centuries of expansion and success. And rather than being seen to be expressions of the so-called criminal mind, these plans of action and gems of counsel are presented for what they indeed are: the reflection of a penetrating understanding of the dynamics of human nature.

One hears in *The Mafia Manager* echoes of Machiavelli, of course, one of the great theorists on the exercise of power. It was Machiavelli, author of the most celebrated treatise yet written on leadership and statecraft, *The Prince*, who counseled the Medicis thusly: "A man who wishes to make a profession of goodness in everything must necessarily come to grief among so many who are not good. Therefore, it is necessary to learn how not to be good, and to use this knowledge and not use it, according to the necessity of the case." We will have recourse to Machiavelli's wisdom as put forth in *The Prince* and in his *Discourses* as we proceed in this guide to success.

Dip into *The Mafia Manager* anywhere at any time and you will find useful advice. Or read it sequentially and slowly, and many times, until its axioms and strategies become an instinctive part of your management equipment—both for corporate climbing and for use in the equally treacherous world at large.

The world at large today, as in its past, turns on greed and fear. Citizens of the United States of America particularly, looking back on their country's last half century especially, and into its next, know this—or should. When you have assimilated the lessons of *The Mafia Manager* you will have learned a central truth: If you think and act solely for your own benefit, you will reach the top. And as the philosopher Nietzsche observed: "On the heights it is warmer than people in the valleys suppose, especially in winter."

As we all know, there's plenty of room at the top— though never enough to sit down.

The
Mafia Manager

Part I
Managing Yourself

Getting There

The best way to enter *our* business is to be born into it. If your father is made and he sponsors you for membership, you're in, although to advance more quickly up the corporate bone heap, or whacking order, you should have an impressive résumé or rap sheet of accomplishments prior to. You should at least have a reputation as a hard-ass and stand-up guy on the street or in the joint. A brother, uncle, cousin, in-law, friend, or acquaintance can also sponsor you if he is a made member, but you'll have to do the scutwork yourself before you can rise. And until you're made—ritually invested into the business/fraternity/family—you're only connected, an affiliate, and not a full member of This Thing of Ours.

As you probably know, This Thing of Ours is a confederacy of crime families throughout the world with a clearly defined hierarchy of members with one aim only: profit, and not averse to using any means to ensure and increase that profit. The Mafia originated in Sicily about five centuries ago, beginning as a patriotic, nationalist organization, but quickly turning to crime. Here in the United States it took on its present form around 1930, shaped by that master administrator of underworld affairs, Johnny "The Fox" Torrio. (Torrio is the man who brought Al Capone to Chicago.)

What does "Mafia" stand for? It stands for honor, vengeance, and solidarity. As an acronym it might stand for

We specialize in protection, dispute resolution, and maintaining orderly markets, especially in those transactions where the state might try to interfere. Internationally, at present, we remain strong in Sicily and are expanding our mission to encourage reason in commercial dealings to Russia. That is Our Thing. Unfortunately, the law sometimes considers our activities to be on its wrong side, that is, illegitimate.

As for This Thing of *Yours*—the legit corporate/business world—it's not all that different from This Thing of Ours (except that you retire from ours only when you retire from living). The rudiments are the same. Obviously, you must first find a position in the world from which you begin to manage your way to the top—that is, the right job. To secure such a job, assess your strong points—education, experience, skills, personality, connections. Then list these in a narrative résumé, emphasizing both the quality and quantity of your past accomplishments and character (as evidenced by awards, honors, fellowships, extracurricular activities and offices and such if you're fresh out of school). A little puffery is not uncalled for.

List for yourself, and yourself alone, your perceived weak points. Prepare yourself to make virtues of these if by any chance they are touched upon in interviews. On your own, work to eliminate them. (In Our Thing, we often help people eliminate major flaws in themselves by eliminating the source itself.)

Learn everything you can about the prospective employers who interest you and use this knowledge every chance you find when you write them, contact them by phone, or interview in person.

Dress up the cover letters you send out with your résumés, dress up the follow-up notes you send out after interviews—that is, use good paper stock, clean, sharp typing. On the follow-ups add a personal line of some sort in your handwriting below your signature.

If you know anything about potential rivals for the position you are seeking, contrive to eliminate these individuals from consideration with faint praise, whether praise is merited or not. If the rivals are competent individuals, worth having as subordinates later on, you can always hire them then, after you've climbed a few pyramid levels above them.

When you secure the job you want, send notes of thanks to all the other prospective employers you interviewed. It doesn't cost a bit more to be nice, and you never know. . . .

Beginner's rules are simple in both your thing and ours: Keep your mouth shut, your eyes open, your fly zipped, and do what you're told. Naturally, as in any business, beginners are required to kiss ass—that is, as someone remarked in another connection, you must have the morals of a whore and the manners of a dancing master—but as time goes by, and you advance, these imperatives will become fewer, until finally you become the guy presenting your cheek to be bussed, which is (presumably) your objective, as (come to think of it) it is the objective of all of us, in one fashion or another.

While you're young, educate yourself by observing the real world, learning what it is and how the real people in it act and react. Remember: Keep your eyes open, your mouth shut. Shape yourself, acquire the tools; eliminate as nearly as possible the traits you have that will hinder you. This will require great effort in the beginning; later on, not so.

Capos

everyone, early in his or her career, needs the sponsorship of a *capo*—a patron, a priest, a rabbi, a mentor. That is, before you can command, you must learn to obey. (Never keep a subordinate of your own who has not learned to obey, no matter how competent otherwise. Never—*especially* if that subordinate is competent.)

When the capo blows, you bend in that wind or break.

When the capo gets hot, you stand there and sweat.

When the capo laughs, you smile (at the very least).

All of this by way of saying, when you are in a subordinate position, you behave like a subordinate. But don't raise your capo's suspicions by being too obsequious. Excessive ass-kissing may be the kiss of death. That is, to be excessively polite is the ultimate rudeness.

When meeting with your capo, speak when spoken to, and then to *his* point; otherwise, stand quiet. If asked for additional information on a subject, provide it if you have it—but only if it's asked for or is extremely vital. In other words, *in fondo*, you are a servitor to a liege lord, or the next thing to it, so long as you remain an underling.

There is an Italian saying *"Tratta con quelli che sono miglio de ti e fagli,"* which means, roughly, "Associate with those better than you and pay full expenses." This defines your relationship to your mentor. No task he gives you is too mean or too bloody (metaphorically speaking) that you would hesitate to undertake it. He is important

to your future, and you must show him that you understand
and appreciate that. You must show him respect.

Later in your career, if by bad happenstance the mentor
of your early years with the company stands in the way
of your own advancement, what do you do? Whack him,
no question. He's had his career, right?

Mentors have authority and power (which is what *you*
want). Doesn't matter how they got them or whether they
deserve them—they got it. They are people with clout and
they will use their clout for you if you do their dirty work.
Al Capone's mentor in Chicago was Johnny Torrio.
(Between the two of them, either could have said of their
adopted city, in the succinct phrasing of one of their most
illustrious countrymen: "Veni, vidi, vici.")

If the capo you report to is a *buffone*, do not show him
up; he will do that himself. So far as you are concerned,
he may not always be right but for now he is your capo.

Demonstrate to him that you are a smart and enterprising
thief and scamster in the company's politicking, but don't
fuck with him or his people, or his associates, or businesses
or institutions under his protection. Do find out who's who
and what's what, storing this information for your own
future use. And above all, never *ever* get your meat where
you get your bread.

If the man you report to is capable, follow his lead,
support him, let him protect you, support you, finance
you, carry you in his wake, and—to repeat—leave his
women alone—wife, mistress, daughters, nieces, cousins,
maids, hookers, secretaries, whatever. But if you're lucky
enough to marry a capo's daughter or close relative—after
first, of course, long before, having received his permission,
verified several times over several weeks, to give her even
so much as a lingering look and a phone call—then count
yourself lucky. (If, however, you should marry a so-called
Mafia Princess, then God help you; no one else can.)

Be sure you understand what your boss has ordered
before you act on his command. What if you whack the
wrong guy, or bomb the wrong joint, or undercut the

wrong assistant at the KC branch office? Learn the art of asking questions; it is easy for some, difficult for others— but always necessary.

Also, don't put anything incriminating in writing— names, addresses, amounts owed, confidential agreements; such documents often wind up as exhibit A in the trials of hapless schmucks, a type you don't want to wind up as. And remember, all capos—just like you—had to start at the bottom, and all stand on the shoulders of giants. On the bones of giants too. When you climb the pyramid, you climb a boneheap. But he who would have the fruit must climb, eh?

Office Politicking

In our business the politicking is done over cups of coffee and months, sometimes years of BSing on hunting trips, during wedding receptions, funerals, golf games, deep-sea fishing or gambling outings, whatever, wherever, mostly social—mostly. Then, when the time seems ripe, or someone gets a wild hair, things happen. Before you know it, so-and-so's driver, say, has moved into the passenger's seat and into so-and-so's position in the organization and so-and-so himself has retired somewhere, either to his own very private plot or, if he's lucky, to his suburban estate, where there's a lot more open space and grass, to play with his grandchildren. Or maybe so-and-so just disappears as if swallowed by the sea, or in a puff of smoke, along with his car and a few of his *compares*.

The thing is, before you could even qualify to become so-and-so's chauffeur (thus entitling you to work for further promotions), you'd have had to become a made member of This Thing of Ours—and to become eligible for that, you'd have had to have made your bones—that is, a whack job, followed by field work in waste disposal (sewer work, undersea concrete work, etc.—disappearing work, *per cosi dire*).

You get the idea, don't you? And before you say "Not for me," be assured you're wrong. Before you are going to become eligible for the big promotions in your business, you *are* going to have to make your bones, in one fashion

or another, just like all the rest of us poor suckers. Which
brings us back to office politicking, the arena where you'll
likely make your bones, and the single most important
office activity you'll be involved in while you're moving
up.

Maybe you've taken one of these helpful Sunday supplement or tabloid quizzes that claim to tell you whether you
have what it takes to become a manager. True or false
questions like "I feel at ease making decisions," or "I'm
always brimming with new ideas," or "I learn from my
mistakes," or "I enjoy meeting people."

How'd you do? ... Forget it. On those quizzes, your
airhead aunt could blitz Julius Caesar and it's unlikely
your aunt is ever going to wield a blade in a knife fight,
which is what managing can be like at times. But then, he
who cannot endure the bad will never see the good.

To become a manager—your thing or ours—one attitude
and one attitude alone is necessary: In every instance, you
look out for the main chance for yourself, and if that means
cutting someone else's throat, that's exactly what it means
you do.

All right, let's get into office politicking. Office politics
are secret and dirty and there is never an end to it. In
your business politicking probably takes place beginning
around the water cooler or in the johns or at some after-
work watering hole—mostly social—but over much
shorter spans of time than in ours. The results, however,
can be almost as disruptive.

As a matter of tactics, there is one overall guide, and
you should carry it up with you when you've gone beyond
politicking at groundling level to judging it from on high
(and making it work for you there as well): To survive, be
patient—watch, listen, and say little; to win, be patient—
survive, plan, and then strike swiftly. You must be sure
to correct or quash any rumor or innuendo that attaches
itself to you.

To put participation in office politics in terms of survival
may at first seem extreme to you. It shouldn't. There is

always at least one friendly office mate out there looking to do you in—always, whether you think so or not, and you must know about him/her to defend yourself. You learn about him through the grapevine, and you take heed, then, and do unto him as he would do unto you, and you do it before he makes his move.

But in the meanwhile, be a friend to every man, woman, or mailroom boy in every office clique that exists, joining none. Make no long-term, close friendships with any colleague, but be cordial to all. Don't dress in a way markedly different from your coworkers, don't act in an offbeat way, even occasionally, and don't tell stories about the wild and crazy personal life you lead after work hours. In other words, don't stand out; fit in.

And don't become involved in any office political battle without first asking yourself, "What's in it for me?" and then "What's in it for them?," and coming up with answers that satisfy you. These two questions should be your *provo dell'acido*—your acid test—with respect to any involvement. In anything.

Most battles you will want to sit out. After all, so what if they're going to stagger the secretaries' lunch hours and the secretaries are up in arms about this arbitrary interference in their lives? What's that to you? You may consider it one of the minor injustices of life also, but at this level in your business career bear in mind that the company doesn't give a damn about you (either). Like each secretary, you too are an easily replaceable part. Sign a petition on behalf of the secretaries and you may well be cutting short a promising career: your own. Remember, every firefly is not a fire.

Perhaps at your present level it hasn't been adequately demonstrated to you how arbitrary, shortsighted, deceitful, petty, spiteful, and completely, irrevocably stupid most of the top management of most companies is. Believe it. We deal with them all the time. Top management. Yup. The higher an ape climbs, the more he exposes his bald ass.

Usually, the older and bigger a company is, the more

unfair it is—from your perspective. From ours, and theirs (the big company's), what's fairness got to do with business? In fact, most of the biggies make Our Thing look like a congregation of followers of Mother Teresa. One example: We *always* tell our people about the risks in our business: death or the joint. The big companies—our country's proud-as-peacocks corporations—tell you nothing except lies. If they tell the truth to those below, it happens by accident. The most you can do if you are employed by one of these firms is tolerate—what should we call it—the moribund and meretricious ambience, and look for the main chance.

Tolerate, survive, lie low; the fall of senile emperors is always just around the corner, and during and after that fall a thousand opportunities wait to be seized. Remember, the hunter's surest weapon is patience.

Listen and learn, and keep marching in to accept those (pitifully small) raises (considering what top management is dragging down). Do it with a smile, or—if you want to be a candy-ass—keep a work journal (as many how-to-succeed books recommend) and use it to justify asking for a bigger raise. You know, a *work journal*, where you log in your completed projects and how much you've accomplished with them, and how much you've saved or made for the company through them.

You may get slightly larger raises with a work journal (but you'll never get the killer promotions with it); or you just may get a can tied to your tail because of it. What is your journal, after all, but a reflection on your supervisor? ("Whaddaya think—I don't *know* what you been doing the past six months?") At the most, send your supervisor a memo when you complete a project, just to put it in the paper record and to pay him/her the compliment of assuming he/she can read. (Of course, in Our Thing, nothing goes down on paper in intelligible form except *pappagallo* droppings.)

Meanwhile, office politicking again, you are doing your job like a good soldier, and keeping your mouth shut, reinforcing alliances where you can, pocketing markers, grabbing turf by getting work out—you and your people— your own work and that of others when they get jammed up or fall down on a project or somehow, mysteriously, have their projects sidetracked to you.

The more allies you have, the more sources of information that are available to you, and information is vital to you. And remember, it pays (or you pay, in a variety of coin) to get information from the enemy, or from the neutrals, or even from your bosses. And what you can't buy, you can steal (but don't get caught), and what you can't buy or steal, you can beat out of someone, metaphorically, of course. . . . Of course.

The reason you play the game of just-one-of-the-fellas (or gals) is to ensure a steady flow of info from all sides. The office grapevine is the most highly reliable source of information available to you (once you winnow out the chaff), certainly ten times as reliable as interoffice memos or pep talks from higher management. Top management often (for no discernible reason) conceals what it does know (even when it has to lie), and more often does not know what middle management is contemplating, anyway (though middle management secretaries always know). Highest management in most companies is insulated from the employees and, even if it were told what was going on, would not listen. (Not listening—not hearing—is an ingrained trait of top management. Not listening even to themselves.)

Along the way in your rise, you'll be handed a dead-end project, a no-win, surefire blank. It happens to us all. If there is any way in the world for you to slough this project onto someone else ("Jim has always been interested in that. In fact, I think he told me he was going to take a night course in it next spring."), do it. That is, if you don't see the end of the road, send someone else. But if it proves impossible to shake, do the best you can with it. You will accrue some small gain: a sense of obligation (a marker) from the higher-up who dumped the dud in your lap.

(Sometimes it is better to take a loss than make a gain—especially when you have no choice.)

Meanwhile, you are making sure your unit's productivity is noticed within the company. Your capo is talking about you and your abilities to higher-ups, you are hitting lower and middle management with short, seemingly in-line-of-duty memos that are actually PR releases on your own behalf, you are friends with most in the office, from high to low, allies with some, a member of no clique but sympathetic to all—and right now, just when everything seems jake—is when you're most likely to find out who your enemies are.

Let's say you've just spent three months on temporary assignment at the Kansas City branch, where you were sent to gut a marketing unit staffed with long-term and thus overpaid deadweights. A few popcorns would have been all right but KC had nothing but people who'd retired on the payroll, and simply firing them outright could have led to legal complications, so your assignment was to accomplish their voluntary departure.

This you did by loading them with work and refusing to okay needed additional help, invariably greeting their sometimes (falsely) cheery comments on the workload with a long face, and switching instructions and deadlines on them. They left like lemmings.

The few holdouts you ran into you put on probation (one had twenty-eight years of service), and even if a man has both oars out of the water he can still hear the rapids crashing ahead, so they too found employment elsewhere.

When you left KC you were friendless but satisfied, since you had successfully completed your assignment. (Such assignments are a little like our going to the joint for the Boss: a pain in the ass but ultimately rewarding. In Our Thing, the Boss helps frame you—with your active cooperation, of course—and takes care of your family while you do his time and stand up—that is, refuse to flip, or stool, or rat, or roll over on him. Being a stand-up guy is a quality highly prized by Men of Honor.)

You return to discover, from various of your informants, that because you are a rising star you have incurred the (usually impersonal) enmity of the most logical rival in your department. (This information is not always delivered straight out, but even when the informant is dissembling you can glean useful information from the nature of the lie told and the manner in which it is delivered). You have foreseen this as a possibility and planned for it.

A caution here: Your rival may be a gnomish, bag-eyed, gray-skinned, mustachioed, loud-mouthed, egomaniacal *cretino*, but you have never let on to him that you feel this way. Instead, you have fed his ego, acted as if you wished to be his friend.

You begin your countermoves before your rival has time to make his move. *A mano a mano*—little by little—into the grapevine:

"Do you think Jay's looking awfully tired lately? I keep wondering if maybe he's got too much on his plate."

"I don't know if it's true or not, but I heard Jay has been offered a sweet deal by XYZ. He'd be hard to replace!"

And to your mutual supervisor: "Jay's staff sure let him down on that last project. But you've got to admire his loyalty to them."

And, finally, the coup de grace setup to Jay's trusted gofer (the weasel who lied to you): "Well, I've had it here. Don't let this get around, but I'm going over to XYZ first of next month."

On the run, Jay takes this confidential news to your department head—as a proven fact. A day later there is a confrontation in your department head's office, at which you produce a copy of your letter to XYZ that firmly rejects their offer. (That is, assuming they made one; doesn't matter—you have a "copy" of your rejection letter, in any case.)

Several days later you learn from the department head's secretary that Jay was summoned to the department head's office and castigated for his lack of "team spirit," and that the lying, egomaniacal *cretino* was told he was not the type of individual your company wants in its employ. "Imagine—one employee trying to hamstring another, and with a falsehood at that!" (In Our Thing, we usually don't bother with the castigation unless the employee is salvageable; if not, we cut to the bottom line.)

You have listened, laid low, produced, kept pocketing markers (which will always be good), kept grabbing turf, and made your bones. Hey! Things happen. *Il buon tiempo verra*—the good time will come.

But still—believe nothing and be on your guard against everything.

Business

The business of the Mafia is business.

We don't like to hurt people, bust balls, break thumbs, smash kneecaps, kick ass. What the hell, in many instances to gain friends we give people lots of money. What could be more American than that? We just want our way when we want it. If a person understands that and cooperates, there won't be any trouble. You fuck with us, though, there's no remedy in the courts, through the cops, through Congress, the Senate, or any other part of government. You've heard of Toys "Я" Us? Well, the Government "Я" Us. We own it, and control it. What we don't own and/or control isn't worth wasting time on. One of ours once said wisely many years ago: "We're bigger than U.S. Steel." I can guarantee you, pal, we're a lot bigger than that today.

How'd this happen? . . . The old-fashioned way. People working with and for people through the *old values*—that's what it's all about, isn't it? Thank God people are people. Their human nature is predictable. They respond to stimulus and incentives. They still believe in the old values. Of these, of course, the chief ones are greed and fear.

Some *basic principles* of business:

Do business with strangers as if they were brothers and with brothers as if they were strangers.

The most important thing in your business relationships is a reputation for honesty. If you can genuinely and sincerely fake honesty, you'll be a success, never doubt it.

What belongs to us is whatever we can take—and keep. Asking costs more than buying, and buying costs more than taking. A handful of might is worth ten times a truckload of right. In business, the Golden Rule is: Whoever has the most power makes the rules and takes the gold.

If the pot is boiling over, use a long spoon. If the house is on fire, warm yourself.

Mind your own business, but keep your eye on other successful businesses. If your neighbor gets up early, you get up earlier.

Never give business advice to another that doesn't profit you and your own interests.

And never act on business advice given you without getting second and third opinions. Your trusted partners and associates may want to see you fail, so be wary.

Sadly enough, if you're too successful, the government takes notice. And if you're unsuccessful, you wind up in the hole. (Many a fuckup in our business has started down the road to success and literally wound up under it.)

The trend in our business—just as in any other visionary contemporary enterprises—is the acquisition of or merger with other successful businesses. And often this can be accomplished only after much adversarial struggle. You've heard of the hostile takeover? We pioneered it. In the free enterprise system, it's big thieves hanging the little ones, all the time.

Regrettably, some of both our friendly and hostile takeovers have eventuated in the bankruptcy of the target company. And some executives of the companies in question also have wound up as casualties.

And yet our principles are the highest: honor, vengeance, solidarity. We know there is no justice for us except as we enforce it. We earn respect.

1 9   Keep these things in mind as you climb the ladder of
success. On the back of your sweatshirt as you climb, there
will always be a stenciled bull's-eye. And: He that seeks,
finds . . . but sometimes what he would rather not, isn't it
so?

Problems

It may take a long time, but with patience even a really serious and persistent problem eventually will go away of itself.

That is, all problems resolve themselves, given time. But often—especially with major problems—self-resolution is so indeterminate and far in the future that you will want to avoid it and try to control what happens.

For major problems, posit the worst possible outcomes. If you can afford those, proceed—at the same time proceeding also to strive to circumvent those worst possible outcomes.

Do not ever base your plans on achieving the best possible outcome, but if it comes, welcome it—after you have examined its every side. What the hell—if heaven drops a plum, open your mouth.

Of course, extreme problems usually require extreme solutions.

Your biggest problems always will originate, as they have from the times of our founders, and from time immemorial, for that matter, from people. There are, *in fondo*, really only two kinds of people: those who take bribes and those who give them. Be a giver—of many kinds of bribes. You can buy friends and allies and soldiers and lieutenants, you know. At least, up to a point. (Enemies you get for nothing.)

Many things in life are beyond our control, but with

people it is usually possible to pull the strings, manipulate them. This does not *always* work, however, and when it doesn't it sometimes precipitates a colossal failure. Sometimes such a failure can bring down an entire family or institution. Look what happened to the Temple when Samson got hold of its pillars.

So the prudent manager always will concentrate his efforts on keeping his people happily well bribed, keeping them in line, keeping them loyal, and keeping them deaf, dumb, and blind—in a manner of speaking, of course.

People problems sometimes must be dealt with harshly. The lesson in this is for others as much as it is for the errant employee. When you make an example of someone, make sure that everyone knows what the lesson is. Punish one, teach a hundred.

It is proper to delude others, but never yourself. That is, as you work your manipulations, never become so caught up in them that you lie to yourself. If you eat it at supper, don't think you can have it for breakfast. Or as one of our own very aptly phrased it: "Shit ain't roses."

When stumped for a solution to a particularly difficult problem, look to the past for a solution. Torrio, Capone, Luciano, Costello, Genovese, Accardo, and others of ours— and some independents we tolerated—were organizational and managerial wizards. Embellish upon their methods. Adapt them to the requirements of your circumstances. (Just don't make the mistake they did.)

What *was* the key to their managerial wizardry, their organizational genius? One thing and one thing only: Their own people feared them as much as their adversaries did. It is said in solemn tones in almost every management text you can find that "respect" is the key to managing people. (And thus solving problems.) In a sense, this is true: Fear is the highest form of respect.

Shortly before he went to prison for income tax evasion, Al Capone explained to an interviewer how he kept the Chicago Outfit running efficiently: "People who respect nothing dread *fear*. It is upon *fear*, therefore, that I have built up my organization. But understand me correctly, please. Those who work *with* me are afraid of nothing. Those who work *for* me are kept faithful, not so much because of their pay as because they know what might be done with them if they broke faith.''

Develop a spectrum of responses to people problems, ranging from an avuncular talking-to all the way up past a vigorous chewing-out, deprivation of income, to mayhem and the ultimate—solving a problem by whacking it. Punishment as a solution, however, has to be exercised with restraint. You must avoid compounding the problem by pushing it into the arms of the competition or the cops— local, county, state, feds, or board of directors.

The mistake the founders made were errors of judgment prompted by that single simple human and classic cause: pride. Men stumble on stones, not mountains.

Time Management

Work smarter, not harder.

Get others to do as much as they can for you.

Hanging out and talking BS is also work, or much of it can be. (But, fellas, let's speak more plainly—you ever listened to those government tapes they play at our trials? How the hell can *we* understand what we're mumbling to each other? Develop a code so that Uncle can't understand what we're saying, then talk all you want. But be sure *you* understand.)

Still, we may do some punching in our business, but we don't punch a clock. Our work often requires that we do a lot of waiting around bored witless between jobs, okay. So may yours. Make that time pay for itself. Read or study something other than the *Racing Form*. Listen to audio-tapes on self-help or help-yourself subjects. The point is, do something, anything, besides sitting there in the Social Club playing cards, bragging about broads, talking scores and scams. All that has its place, and courtesy requires that you bullshit with your peers and colleagues, but not for months on end and nothing else. Just as well to have no time as to make no good use of it.

Because our line of work attracts ambitious, lazy people, the young man who wants to move up will find productive work for his spare time that attracts the notice, fills the pocket, reinforces the power, adds to the glory of his superiors. Find such a sideline for yourself.

Choose the time of day or night when your energies are highest and conduct business at that time. We receive business associates, petitioners, visitors only at that time when we are at our best. Mistakes in our line of work may eventuate in death or the joint, so we're careful—we try to do things at the right time. We make our rounds, our collections, issue our threats, kick ass, bust heads, and smile at friend and/or foe alike when the time is right. You do the same. Not a minute sooner or later. If you must do something at a time inconvenient for you, be less than brief, say less than nothing, do nothing more than show up and reschedule.

But remember, effective time management is not the rigid establishment of a routine. Scheduling is not a fixed, one-time act, nor is long-range planning. After all, who knows what or who will turn up, roll over, or take a fall? Plus the other daily hassles that cause us all grief beyond belief.

The best thing to invest in your business is your time. To schedule, plan, and use time effectively, know your turf and know your objectives. Assess the obstacles and opportunities, then devise your strategies.

Some of our basic time-saving strategies:

We always double park.

We don't spend an hour roughing up and shaking down a guy for a measly two hundred. We have lawyers who make more than that who rarely work up even a mild sweat.

We don't do anything ourselves that we can pay, con, or order someone else to do.

Some of us set our watches behind ten minutes. Why should we show up early at a meet or sitdown and have to wait for other people? We let them wait for us. Unless they're our superiors. In which case, we're on time, no question.

We have a change of clothing wherever we hang out regularly—club, gym, favorite joints, girlfriend's place, wherever. Then we always have fresh clothes and don't have to waste time buying, stealing, or going back home for something clean to wear.

In our business, especially if we are a subordinate, we are on twenty-four-hour call. Any hour of the night or day the phone may ring and we'll have to move. Even if it's our day off or we're on vacation, business comes first, before anything else. If we're running some sideline business on our own, then that comes second. Nothing gets in the way of these two, not even the wife or girlfriend.

There are many kinds of time, including the time you do in the joint. Joint time you do one day at a time; you *build* time. When you do something for a superior, you do it quickly. When you do a favor for a subordinate, you do it, but there's no particular hurry. When you have to do something for the cops or the government, then you do it when you can't do anything else to avoid doing it. When we have to do something, but it's not for our superiors, subordinates, family, friends, business associates, cops, or G, then we do it whenever we're damn good and ready.

These basic tenets of effective time management set forth, here are some nuts and bolts for use where *you* work. But don't forget the basics.

Effective time management means making the most of every minute you work—and making certain that you have hours every day and days every week, weeks and weeks every year when you do not have to work. The last is what the objective of effective time management for everyone but the workaholic should be. Work smarter, we said, not harder.

The three basic rules of effective time management are:

1. Schedule your tasks.
2. Delegate them.
3. Delegate more of them.

Lecturers at seminars on management expound on creating the "ideal work space" as an aid to time management, creating "quiet" time, minimizing distractions and interruptions. improving decisiveness, streamlining time, and so on. Their strategies become very complicated as they seem to offer techniques to add a twenty-fifth hour to your day. Thing is, you could spend a good year just getting set up to start on them.

As with most matters of management, however, time management can be reduced to common sense. If you know how to manage time, you need at the most only six hours in your day, and those not every day.

The ideal work space is wherever it is you've found you work best. This may be in a booth at the corner coffee shop, a table in the kitchen of your house, an otherwise vacant office at your place of business—wherever distractions and interruptions are least and you feel comfortable.

Choosing the time of day—or night—when your energies are at their highest, as we said earlier, you sit there with a cup of coffee or tea and let your mind roam. Surprise!— your mind will begin to plan and to generate solutions to problems. You have found—"created"—both the ideal work space and "quiet" time.

Take a yellow legal pad and draw a line down the middle. (Date the sheet at the upper right.) In the left column block out what needs to be done (in a shorthand only you understand), ranking the tasks equivalent with their payoff and urgency, balancing the two, one against the other, as you assign and review the tasks' priority.

You have scheduled.

Next, in the right-hand column, assign the tasks to others wherever possible.

You have delegated.

Then appraise and reappraise the two columns, reassigning priorities where it seems wise or necessary, delegating further.

Keep at it until your mind suggests no further additions or revisions.

You have assigned tasks to yourself, more to others, in the order of their apparent importance. Tomorrow you will check off what's been accomplished and begin a new two-column sheet for the day (destroying the old), revising, assigning, reassigning. This is effective time management. It is also the art of delegation.

Key a similar sheet for the week and one for long-range objectives. Might as well begin today; it is too late to fetch the salt once the meal is eaten.

But remember, as we said: Scheduling is not a fixed, one-time act, nor is long-range planning. Both are processes of constant adjustment, given life's contingencies. Be flexible. This is something the old Mustache Petes—the earliest *mafioso* in the United States, direct from the old country—knew well, up to a point—and then, past that point, they got overly pleased with the way things were going for themselves and forgot it. . . . The Mustache Petes are long dead and gone. That's the lesson.

To schedule and plan, you must know your objectives, both qualitatively and quantitatively. Suppose you set yourself this grandiose long-range objective: *Retire at forty with $1 million.* You must then assess the obstacles and opportunities and devise your strategies and tactics, always bearing in mind your resources and the risks involved. And then you plan how to do it: who does what, in what sequence, and where, and with what, and how. This gives you your action plan, the set of tasks to be accomplished in what time frame.

And then, as before, you delegate.

Now let's say you work in an organization that requires you to show up and be there for office hours of nine to five. The art of time management here is to keep your office door closed, permitting entry only to those you want to see, when you want to see them.

Your secretary is the gatekeeper. If someone on your staff should get past her and pop his head in unannounced and say, "Busy?" you reply with a menacing "Yes!"

When you do meet with a staff member in your office and the staffer has a lot on his mind or is a gabber, or both, but you've already found out what you need to know, pull

some papers to you from across your desk, bend your head
to them, and say, "Well, thanks. I've got to get some work
done now." Meeting over.

Unless you're the kind of person who prefers to answer
his own phone calls (some managers do: up-to-the-minute
information straight from the earpiece), give your secretary
the names of those callers you will speak to at once when
they call (make it a short list) and instruct her to take
messages from the rest. At about the same time every day,
sit down and return those calls you think are important
as well as those you want to. Callers who don't hear from
you will call again.

If you return a call and the words from the other end of
the line go on endlessly (that is, to no end), hang up and
proceed to your next call back. Very few people will believe
that you hung up on yourself, preferring for their pride's
sake to blame AT&T. If you've used this tactic recently on
the same caller, try silence. Don't respond. Nothing. Quite
soon your caller will nervously end his one-sided conversation himself. If the caller is *very* important but you want
to end the conversation, tell him you have a scheduled
appointment, right then.

Your closed door doesn't, and should not, prevent you
from wandering the halls and cubicles of the office at will,
when it suits you, spreading cheer and fear among your
staff and finding out who is doing what to whom and why
and what the hell is really getting done.

Decision Making

Before making an important management decision, get as much as you can of the best information available—even if you have to beat it out of someone—and review it carefully. Discuss it with other wiseguys, analyze it, draw up worst-case scenarios, add up the plus and minus factors, discuss it with your *consiglière*, then do what your gut tells you to do. The man with a great gut—*per cosi dire*, an instinct for the right move at the right time—will go to the top in any business. When your gut fails you on a major move, however, it could mean death or the joint. (Note that this is a recurring theme in our business, and all decisions must be calculated with this death-or-the-joint factor built into the equation. It probably would be correct to assume that the penalty for failure in your business is not as drastic.)

With less important decisions, identify the problem, gather the facts, pose the solutions, and try to foresee their consequences, keeping in mind that every *maybe* has a *maybe not*. Consult with others, including your *consiglière*.

Then put the problem out of your mind for a time. Your subconscious will work on it, and, often enough, the correct decision will come to you by itself, without your working at it consciously. Yes, it sounds as bad as going to, say, an astrologer to tell you what to do, but believe it or not, it works, and it works most of the time. It is, in fact, what the person with the great "gut" for decisions relies on.

To review, concerning a decision, get the best information you can into your head. Check it out with others. Think about it. Then decide on the basis of what your gut tells you.

That is, to make a decision, large or small, discover, examine, and consider the following:

1. The specific nature of the problem
2. The facts or what seem to be the facts
3. The alternatives and their possible consequences or rewards

Then solicit the views of others, let your subconscious do its work—and make your decision.

Look back only to evaluate the results and garner from them knowledge for future use.

And always, always save your lottery tickets.

Finally, if after everything you should still make a bum decision, do what we all do—your thing or ours: Blame the failure on someone else and move quickly to mete out appropriate correction and/or punishment.

Friends

Friends are never as important as family. Do not confuse the loyalty of friendship with the bond of blood. Friends you can buy with a variety of coin. Family is forever, thick or thin, feast or famine, *fino alla fescia*, to the bitter end—except for the exceptions. But that's a genetic problem; every family has its share of idiots, cretins, half-wits, defectives, bumblers, drunks, addicts, and traitors. It's inevitable. But they reveal themselves very early, so take necessary precautions. These poor souls are more to be pitied and dealt with than chastised long and loudly, especially since that's usually without result.

The problem with friends is their candor. They'll betray you eventually, if you let them, and then they'll tell you to your face why: "It's nothing personal, just business." They'll always assert their paramount loyalty to money and power with the same line: "Nothing personal, just business."

Your *true* friends you'll know, but not until they are tested. Until then, you can never be sure. So long as things go well for you, that test may never come. There is no help for this except to acknowledge it and act accordingly, never placing all your trust in *anyone* else. A true *mafioso* has no friends, only interests.

Can you buy the friendship and loyalty of another? Five hundred years ago, Machiavelli had this to say about friends and their value to a leader: "For it may be said of men in general that they are ungrateful, voluble, dissemblers, anxious to avoid danger, and covetous of gain; as long as you benefit them, they are entirely yours . . . friendship which is gained by purchase . . . is bought but not secured, and at a pinch is not to be expected in your service."

Some would advise: Do not go into business with friends or their children. Some would advise: Do not lend friends money or borrow it from them. We urge the opposite, however, but with all due caution. Why should a little friendship stand in the way of business? And if you ever have to deal harshly with a friend, you'll know his hangouts and habits, the better to facilitate any action against him you may want to take. Nothing personal, just business.

Never tell your friends how well you're doing—they won't believe you, or will condemn you for bragging. Don't tell them how bad things are going either—they'll gloat and leak word back to your enemies, who may take your misfortune as a sign to move against you. And don't be too quick to believe what your friends say to you about your enemies.

By the time you assume a higher management position, you should have all the friends you need. Friends acquired after you become a top manager are doubly suspect. What you will need more of is allies. You don't necessarily have to like your allies; history is full of appropriate examples.

Enemies

Keep your friends close, but keep your enemies closer.

The most dangerous enemy is a crazy man, a *pazzo*—he cannot be reasoned with, he's not afraid to die, and he doesn't give a damn about the people close to him. He must be destroyed, quickly and thoroughly.

The same holds true in a major showdown with *any* enemy: You must destroy him—otherwise he will start plotting his revenge. What happens to enemies that are not destroyed? Look at Japan and Germany.

Fear your enemies; not to fear them invites disaster.

Look for enemies in unexpected places: under and in your own bed, and in yourself.

One good thing about an avowed enemy: You know who he is.

A man without enemies is a man without qualities. Think not? Even Jesus Christ had many, many enemies.

Always think the worst of your enemies; you will seldom be mistaken. But remember, revenge is a dish best eaten cold.

Axioms

The world belongs to the patient man.

Think much, speak little, write less.

If you can't win by fighting fair, fight foul. Or have a third party do your fighting.

Teach your tongue to say "I don't know."

If you must strike out at someone when you get angry, be careful not to strike yourself.

Fire can be concealed, not smoke.

Much better your enemies think you are crazy than reasonable and rational.

One grain does not fill a sack, but it helps.

He that blows on a fire gets sparks in his eyes.

Hunger changes bread into cake, beans into beefsteak.

Opportunity makes the thief; the thief who has no opportunity to steal considers himself an honest man.

Nothing weighs less than a promise.

He who serves two masters must lie to one. (It is also well known that a pig with two masters soon starves.)

If you must hurt a man, do it so brutally you need not fear his revenge.

Even a mouse keeps three holes.

If you allow your enemies—or friends—to think they are your equals, they will immediately think they are your superiors.

Don't try to change your enemies, just try to control them. Know where they are, what they think, and who they trust.

Promise little; deliver much.

When you are angry, close your mouth—and open your eyes. But don't get angry, get even.

State to yourself what you would be; then do what is necessary.

Never underestimate these three things: (1) your opponent's abilities; (2) your opponent's cunning; (3) your opponent's greed. Never overestimate them either.

He who answers for another pays the bill.

The only way to keep a secret is to say nothing.

Overvalue negative estimates of your prospects in any venture by two. Undervalue positive estimates by half.

Better to cut the shoe than pinch the foot.

All who snore are not sleeping.

If you must lie, be brief.

There is no such thing as coincidence.

Open your mouth and your wallet cautiously.

Study the conventional wisdom, then shun it.

The crow that mimics a sea gull drowns.

What is not known can be forgotten. That is, a weapon not used draws no blood. Nothing for nothing.

The best defense against the treacherous is treachery.

Some defeats are better than victories; unfortunately, some victories are worse than defeats.

Take warning from others of what may be to your own advantage. Give others no warning.

No man's credit is worth as much as his cash.

Often you lose the bait when you catch the fish. This is a necessary loss.

Don't pluck a green apple; when it ripens it will fall of itself.

Always draw the snake from its hole with another man's hand.

Don't use both feet to test the depth of the river.

Those who cannot do as they would must do as they can. What cannot be cured must be endured. Make sure you can do as you would, or do not set that as an objective.

God will provide—but you must provide till He does.

Rashness is the parent of misfortune.

The man who wants to hang himself can always be led to a noose.

Necessity breaks all laws.

A smart street lieutenant does some of the dirty work himself, making certain his soldiers know about it.

If you are forced to bow, bow very, very low. And hold that bitter memory until you take your revenge.

It takes a thousand blows to drive a nail in the dark.

Never trouble trouble till trouble troubles you.

Stick to what you know best. Trees often transplanted seldom prosper.

Never knock someone else's racket. (You never know when you may be pulling the same stunt yourself some day.)

Boldness in business is the first thing—and the second—and the third.

Establish priorities: If you're up to your ass in alligators, the first thing to do is drain the swamp.

Everything in the world is quid pro quo.

A thousand friends are not enough; a single enemy is. There is no such thing as a "harmless" enemy.

Let your adversary help you. (One way your adversary can help you is by letting his "better" instincts betray him. Permit that.)

Make plans as complex as necessary, but give simple orders.

If you can't win, make the price of your enemy's victory exorbitant.

Be civil to all, sociable to many, familiar with a few, and friendly to a handful.

He is a fool that cannot conceal his wisdom.

A homely girl will always laugh at your jokes.

The best armor is to keep out of range.

When a bet is made, be sure you hold the stakes.

Your adversary is never as powerful as you may think he is. Neither are you.

The best friend of a hungry buzzard is a dead horse. That is, in another way of saying, even a son of a bitch has his uses.

Part II
Managing
Others

Hiring

nce you're managing people, sooner or later you will have to hire people. This can be an eye-opener, since you will find (once those you hire begin to work for you) that most people are more incompetent than you probably expected—certainly more so than their résumés or they themselves had led you to believe. (Self-praise, of course, is not a recommendation; a monkey in a tuxedo is still a monkey.) Nonetheless, people—with all their failings—are what you have to work with, and on them will depend much of your success as a manager.

It is not necessary to have a large family with many soldiers and button men. In fact, the fewer employees you have, the fewer betrayals or disappointments you will experience. Many employees, many betrayals and disappointments—also, higher overhead.

But your staff must be of the highest possible quality in the critical positions. One good man is, of course, better by far than a hundred fools.

For a truly responsible job involving others in its performance (which most jobs do, even those requiring highly technical skills), don't hire someone just out of school, no matter how impressive his record there. Hire the person who already has demonstrated an ability to work with others. For jobs less critical to the success of your organization, however, you will want to hire a good attitude before experience. (Attitude can reveal itself in a number of ways.

For example, if an applicant asks about salary early on in the first interview, his is a bad attitude; moreover, he is stupid.)

For a truly vital job, don't hire a high-powered expert, no matter how impressive his credentials. Experts care only about their credentials and their fees, and there their caring stops.

Don't hire more than two members of the same household (except, possibly, your own), and never hire lovers or husband and wife, no matter how necessary their individual skills may be to your organization.

Before you hire, you will interview. Knowing what skills and performance you want from the person you will hire, give applicants time to think about your questions on those matters. Be specific in your questioning. Generalities beget general (thus, useless) responses. Require applicants to be specific in their answers. Use the questions "Why?" and "How?" to follow up responses.

As for the interview strategy itself, seat the applicant beside you, if possible, rather than across the desk from you, in order to better gauge his reactions (shifting body, averting eyes, gulping—that sort of thing). Pick up his/her résumé and scan it, frowning now and then as if pondering some obvious flim-flam. This bit of playacting finished, and the applicant suitably unsettled by it, it is to be hoped, begin by asking the applicant why he wants the vacant job and why he feels qualified to do it. Let him sell himself as much as he wants to, interrupting only with specific questions ("How?" "Why?"). Finally, if the applicant is presently working, ask him why he wants to change jobs.

Repeat the last sentence of the reply to this last question as if puzzling some possible deviousness, and then lay out the requirements of the job that's open—stressing difficulties. If the applicant should, say, frown or squirm or stroke his cheek with apparent concern while you're outlining the job's difficulties, you should begin to consider kissing him off. In polite language let your feelings be known to the applicant. Unless he tries to sell himself back into contention ("I've always thrived on tough assignments—that's what I'm looking for"), do kiss him off. Tell him you have others to interview, of course, and you'll let him know, one way or another, in a day or two. If you're fairly sure you don't want to see more of him, muse aloud as you say good-bye that perhaps he's overqualified for the job—and wish him well.

Also kiss off any applicant who's full of questions about his career's future with you. That isn't all he's full of, and you don't want him.

In any case, close interviews when you have found out what you need to know, whether this takes five minutes or fifty.

When an applicant seems worth another look, check out his business references and employment history. Forget about the personal references. He's not going to list someone who will bum-rap him. If you yourself happen to know one or more of his personal refs, however, a call to them may get you some useful inside info.

Bring in the most likely candidate for a second interview, preferably at lunch, and at this meeting zap him with whatever may seem to have turned up bogus in his business references or employment history. If those doubts, real or imagined, are resolved to your satisfaction, sell the job to the applicant. Sell the job; make no promises of future raises, promotions, or broadening of responsibilities. What the applicant gets is what he gets; nobody—not even you—has a crystal ball that works. Let him do the job applied for, then we'll see what happens.

Following your selling of the job, pose a few hypothetical problems the applicant may encounter on the job and ask him how he might go about meeting them. If the applicant passes muster, make an offer and hire him. If not, back to the office to schedule a second interview with the next most likely candidate.

Most applicants will be more relaxed at the second interview and reveal more of their true natures, especially since you're lunching together. Table habits and conversation tell much about a person. (Wine tells all.)

You are looking for quality, of course, but you will, accidentally, sometimes hire bumblers. In fact, there will be applicants who are instantly recognizable as such popcorns. Even so, depending on the nature of the opening you are hiring for, you may want to take a long look at some of these people—just as you may want to promote some bumbler-soldiers you already have to lieutenants. There are slots in every organization that bumblers can fill quite well without severely damaging anything when they periodically fuck up, as they will. (Take a look at the U.S. Postal Service. Half of the USPS workforce are bumblers— a normal percentage in any large organization—and 99 percent of the time with surliness to the customer thrown in . . . and still the mail gets through. The reason it gets through so poorly, however, is not because of the bumblers in the workforce of this huge "service" organization. That reason is deliverable to the USPS top management, which is composed 100 percent of overpaid tap dancers.)

When your own bumbler really screws up, take him aside in private and chew the hell out of him. He will make every effort thereafter to shape up (often by finding or recruiting a capable soldier to do his work for him). Ordinarily, however, a bumbler–on day-to-day duty—can do no more damage than a blind horse in an empty barn.

But why would you hire—even promote and pay well— a *buffone*? There are reasons: Such a person will be one of the most loyal followers you have. Loyal out of gratitude to you for giving him work (and an income), and then keeping him even after it becomes obvious he can't cut it—and loyal out of fear that you may at any time ax him because of his incompetence. He needs your support to stand at all: He exists solely by your sufferance.

Because of his loyalty, the bumbler also will prove to be your most reliable reporter on office politics and other

useful gossip, and it is in this area that his employment
probably pays its biggest dividends.

Such a person also can be good for bopping around with,
and—oh, yes—can be sacrificed with small loss to your
organization, should a sacrifice in some small skirmish
ever be required. Nothing personal.

It should go without saying (but does so only at your
peril) that you never hire someone of the opposite sex in
hopes of future erotic reward, unless all you want to do
is look. But which of us ever stopped there?

Soldiers and Lieutenants

Betrayal is where it's at in the lives of most humans; therefore, all else being equal, loyalty is the paramount quality to be looked for in soldiers and lieutenants. The only person you can ever trust completely—ever, under any circumstances—is yourself. (Thus you can trust yourself to trust others provisionally, if you choose.)

After loyalty come ability, skill, and competence. Promote only able people (and the occasional bumbler). You find able people by testing them. They must make their bones and then proceed to the next, harder tasks you give them.

Having established the competence of a select few, give them increasingly difficult jobs—but jobs you think they can handle successfully—and then praise their success, much as you'd build confidence in a child. Promote them to still harder tasks and give them larger rewards and then ever-harder tasks.

Do not criticize beyond necessity and seldom in public. And always precede criticism with a few words of praise.

Most of your soldiers will have little idea of their own worth (or, for that matter, of their own inferiority). You—through your street lieutenants chiefly—must give them the idea they are worth something. You have to make the tasks you set them matter to them. They must want to do the jobs given them, and they must be able to feel proud of themselves once they have done them. They must, that is, come to see a meaning in their lives because of the work they do for you.

Therefore, you must praise when praise is due (sometimes even when it isn't), and they will work for your success.

Showcase your lieutenants when others are present. This will lead your lieutenants to think themselves most favored. Let your lieutenants think they have done it all themselves; don't let them forget you told them to do it.

Give clear-cut specific directions to your lieutenants and make clear what their reward will be for success. But don't reveal to them what the whole plan for any undertaking is. Since none of your soldiers and lieutenants will know all, they will be very much dependent on you.

Make your soldiers and lieutenants your children.

Consiglière

The best advice makes you think for yourself. Therefore, when choosing a *consiglière*—your senior advisor—select an individual with broad experience and practical views. And, of course, someone you trust.

Traditionally, a *consiglière* is a sounding board, a counselor, someone who advises, someone who can be leaned upon. *Venire a piu miti consigili* means "to become more reasonable." A *consiglière* helps you to do this. He stands at a distance from your immediate, close-up problems and concerns, and from your emotional involvement with them, because the final responsibility is not his. (Neither does he have the ultimate power and authority; that too is yours.) Because he stands at a distance, your *consiglière* can help you identify the nature of large problems and aid you in their analysis and solution. (As one of his lesser duties, the *consiglière* can mediate the smaller disputes within the organization.)

The *consiglière* also can jar you loose from false assumptions, because he is, in a sense, disinterested. Totally interested but, still, disinterested—again because the ultimate responsibility is not his.

You can get bad advice from good friends, very bad advice from very good friends. In contrast, the advice you get from your *consiglière* usually will be very good advice, and it is always worth considering on its considerable

4 9 merits. The best *consiglière* forces you to think and ask questions, and he will usually advise counter to the conventional wisdom because—being of broad experience and practical views—he knows that what everyone else assumes to be true and correct can't be.

Secretary

At the very least, your secretary should be a bodyguard, a gatekeeper, a diplomat, a general, and totally dependent on your generosity and goodwill for her financial and psychological well-being.

Your secretary must be more trustworthy than your spouse. She will know everything you know about your business—with the exception of those of your long-range plans (in their entirety) that you do not choose to confide in her—and many aspects of the business she will know better (in more detail) than you. Additionally, she is close to sources of reliable office gossip and the machinations of office politicking, and will prove a good and accurate source of information for you.

Never, ever ask her to make coffee. Send out for it, so she can have a cup with you when she brings it in.

She is critical to the success of your business plans and can destroy you quicker than your competitors or federal regulations if she should ever want to. Keep her happy. Her enmity is not something you would ever wish to incur. While you're at it, give her a nice title—and responsibility and authority to equal it, as well as a *good* salary.

Romantic involvements with her are, of course, strictly taboo.

Personnel Director

The Mob doesn't have one, why should you?

By the time your organization gets so big that some in it think it needs a personnel director, your department heads will have lost touch with their staffs—a dangerous situation. Managers should recruit and hire their own people.

If you have someone handling the mechanics of personnel, make sure they handle only the mechanics. Never let them write recruiting ads or do first screening. *Never* let them interview job candidates. Managers should recruit and hire their own people.

When you yourself hire someone to work directly for you—a twenty-something who's starting at the bottom—you may want to point out that his/her first assignments will be pure scutwork and that most of what he got in his college classrooms won't apply. Advise him to perform these first tasks willingly and well, even though he feels overqualified. Tell him to sit on the brilliant ideas for improvements in procedures and operations that will occur to him immediately; that they've already been tried and found wanting. Point out that the secretaries and other support staff in your organization are among the most important allies he can make. And counsel him to try to fit in, at least initially, even though he may feel that most of his coworkers are leading dull, plodding personal and work lives compared to his own. In other words, tell him to keep the noise level low.

If you were not talking to a college grad but to a wannabe in Our Thing, you wouldn't have to give such advice; we learn those lessons on the street. But men or women with college educations are at a disadvantage: they've been told they know something and they believe it.

Accountant

Only one person in your organization has to be completely honest, completely forthcoming, completely open and above board, completely incorruptible: the person in charge of keeping your company's books (and your own personal books). Pay him well and reward him often; with praise, if nothing else.

If there is enough work for two or more, hire assistants who would like his job. If there's not enough work for more than one person, have the company's books audited often.

Job Titles

Job titles are extremely important. That's why banks and advertising agencies have so many vice presidents. Important customers want to deal with "someone in authority." Ditto for important insiders within your company. Sometimes an ambitious employee will settle for less of a raise if a fancy job title comes with a promotion. You can use this as a bargaining point. The world lives on pretense. Help it along.

Job titles also can be used as euphemisms for the inevitable menial or unpalatable work that must be done. (A sewer worker becomes a "sanitation engineer.") This softens the pain of the sweat and slurs that go with such jobs.

Some Mob watchers claim that the job title "boss of all bosses" was eliminated because it created jealousy and animosity among the heads of the families. All the bosses wanted to be equal, none wanted to be subordinate—hence the creation of a national commission with a one-man, one-vote policy. The world lives on pretense.

Raises

establish a yearly review policy in which job performance is evaluated against a predetermined percentage limit imposed on maximum increase. If an employee deserves it, give him/her a raise at the yearly review.

You must, of course, reward diligent, hardworking, loyal employees, so in special cases an outstanding worker may be raised above the maximum, at your discretion. But make sure the worker knows how generous you're being by exceeding the wage limitations dictated by your controller, creditors, stockholders, the commission, or whatever dark forces you claim really control your business.

Some workers will never be satisfied, no matter how much money they make. When they complain to you about being underpaid, tell these people that a part-time job—in addition to their full-time work for you—may help them make ends meet. Tell them you encourage such additional employment, if it doesn't interfere with their full-time job performance.

The Organization, in fact, usually does not object to its employees doing a little business on the side to supplement their incomes, providing such business has the prior approval of top management.

Loyalty

▲ll men try to work in their own interests—and most men believe they know what that is (often mistakenly, but never in doubt).

Your job is to make them identify their interests with yours.

You do this by punishing them when they fail, rewarding them when they succeed. You cultivate the loyalties of others by showing them that their profit lies where yours does.

The identification is reciprocal, since they are working at tasks you have assigned them.

But in appraising their achievement, you must be fair. If they "fail" at a task you have set them, perhaps circumstances were uncontrollable—or perhaps you were mistaken in your evaluation of the situation.

Until you decide to terminate a subordinate's employment for the reason of unfitness, weight the scales in that individual's favor and proceed slowly.

One last, important item: *Anyone* in *your* organization is *always* in the right if opposed by an outsider. Even if your soldier is wrong, he is right; that can be straightened out between the two of you later. And you, as boss, are always right to those in your organization, whether opposed by outsiders or, once you've made a decision, questioned by some young Turk or old turkey in your own organization. (Young Turks often become old turkeys.)

Types

If human nature doesn't confuse you occasionally, you don't understand it. It takes all kinds—which is not to say that human beings can't be classified into certain basic types if you don't worry too much about shadings, blends, and simplifications.

There is one category of people you should steer far clear of regardless of what other type category they may fall into: the tap-dancing fine talkers. You are not interested in fine talk from your captains, lieutenants, and soldiers. You are interested only in results; they speak for themselves.

There are many other variants of types—personality categories—you need not be interested in unless they have special skills for special jobs, after the doing of which such people can be dispensed with: the whiner, the hothead, the sniper-shark, the nonstop gossip, the blustering egomaniac—all of these, for instance. The point is, you don't have to employ anyone who is hard to get along with or, for that matter, who parts his hair in a way you don't like. Tie a can to their tail. This is one of the prerogatives of being a manager.

Remember: (1) Nobody hires anybody for anything except to make money for themselves from what that person can do. Nobody, anybody. And (2) there are always at least a dozen people out there who can do the very same thing equally well; you have your choice. No need to be stuck with a know-it-all, say, who rubs you the wrong way.

(This rule of the marketplace holds as well for marital matters and affairs of the heart.) You have people who throw temper tantrums, who sulk, who procrastinate, who gush but don't deliver? Dump them. Probably good for them, ultimately, and best for you, right now.

Basically, then, look to find four types of soldiers in any organization. These are:

1. Dumb and lazy (that is, not ambitious)
2. Smart and lazy
3. Dumb and ambitious
4. Smart and ambitious

The first type—dumb and lazy—usually don't know whether they should shave their ass and scratch their chin or vice versa. These are the sloggers, the bumblers, the tap dancers, and some days it will seem to you that three-fourths of your soldiers are shaving their ass, but the percentage seldom exceeds 50 percent in any organization and is usually about 25 to 30 percent.

If given simple, clearly stated directions, bumblers will perform day-to-day routine tasks well enough, usually will be content with token raises (half or less of cost-of-living increase), and will be among your most loyal employees. They have their uses, which is fortunate, since every organization must employ many of them for lack of better.

The second type—smart and lazy—you should load up on. These people wouldn't spend a penny to watch an ant stack a ton of hay, but they could find a needle in that ton if they had to.

That is, they must be continually prodded and they will produce. You must see to it that your lieutenants keep prodding. They—the smart and lazy—will do most of the upper-level scutwork in your organization.

Many managers regard the smart and lazy as difficult and try to avoid hiring them or keeping them. This is a mistake. They need only be motivated with a sharp stick. Oddly enough—perhaps not so oddly—a *consiglière* is often of this type. He lacks the inner fire to turn his brains into personal power, but he has the brains to do well as an advisor.

The third type—dumb and ambitious—can be recognized by the fact that he/she will be flattering you constantly. The dumb and ambitious believe in using manure on their strawberries, while most of us settle for cream and sugar. Up to a point, this type can be useful, since they work hard to curry your favor. (Thus, they make efficient gofers.) The point where they cease to be useful is reached when their egotism leads them to claim expertise and to accept tasks beyond the capacity of hard work and their bone-deep dumbness.

They are also so insecure that they do not work well for strong, capable lieutenants, nor does their overbearing (usually ill-hidden) conceit endear them to those who may work under them. They want to control, to rule, but they lack the tools.

Finally, for all their flattery of you, they also lack lasting loyalty. This is not to be wondered at, however, since any ambitious person is basically disloyal—he wants to displace the person above him. You know this yourself, about yourself. The dumb and ambitious do not, regrettably, have enough smarts to hold their ambition in check until the time is right to make their move without unduly disrupting the work of the organization. Consequently, the first problem of this nature that one of this type causes— let him out.

A word of caution: A dumb and ambitious soldier (as well as a dumb and lazy soldier, it should be noted) may— in spite of innate stupidity—possess cunning. Those who do, the Germans call *dummschlau*: stupid-smart. Such a soldier is very dangerous in an organization and when discovered should be whacked, because otherwise he will eventually betray you. The *dummschlau* is usually discovered in a small matter, if you're lucky and he is not quite cunning enough. Then you apply the principle "False in one, false in all" and take the appropriate action.

Fourth and last, the smart and ambitious. This type is the individual you give ever-harder tasks to and keep rewarding and promoting when he succeeds. As personalities they can be dour or quiet, touchy or easygoing, grave or pleasant, whatever—but they succeed at what they're given to do and engender success for the organization.

Most men and women, of course, are blends of the four types. You will rarely encounter a person who is a pure representative of any of the four.

Ideally, you want individuals working for you who are deeply loyal to you; who are honorable, direct, courageous, creative, talented, energetic, quiet; who have a record of meeting or exceeding the objectives set for them; who hold themselves and their deeds in the background; who seem to lack jealousy; who seem to think not first of themselves but rather of the goals of the organization (as stated by you); who seem not to grasp for power but who can wield authority when given it.

You will find no such Boy Scouts, but you must look for their approximations; the individuals who come closest to meeting the ideals are those you promote. Promotion itself will tell you more about the person, because power acts like a cancer on human beings; it enlarges their sense of their own worth and wastes away other, better qualities they may have until—with some—at last they have become only their sense of their own worth—sheer, all-encompassing ego.

Those to whom this doesn't happen are the truly exceptional. That's right: You.

Leadership

According to an old Sicilian proverb, the pleasure of commanding is sweeter than sexual intercourse. This may be so.

At any rate, people have tried different styles of commanding—of dealing with subordinates: by showing, by letting subordinates participate, by being a buddy to subordinates, or simply by giving orders. The last is far and away the most reliable and effective. In commanding—handling people—the test of your success is not building trust and credibility, nor is it getting others to like you; the test is achieving your objectives. The test of *their* success is in whether they get the job done. Cut no slack for your staffers, less for yourself.

Before assigning a task, know the facts of the situation and the facts about the staffers who will do the work. Make recommendations and give directions in specific terms with recognizable objectives. Give as few orders as possible.

Know why you are speaking—what you want accomplished. Respond to questions until it is entirely clear what you want done, and never apologize.

Don't be too familiar with your subordinates; it may at first inspire affection, but eventually, like all familiarity, it will breed contempt.

Never accept a confidence about a superior from his subordinate. The day may come when the subordinate

becomes the superior's confidant, and then—knowing
what he has said to you—he may decide to protect himself.

Even the lowest soldier in your family has influence on somebody. To get the maximum effort from all of them, show them respect; but remember, they are not dons.

Regardless of the quality of your staff, you have to keep telling its members how good they are, or can be. You must stress their worth and the value to you of what they do; you cannot praise their successes too often. And if you're going to criticize failures publicly, criticize them as a group; don't single out individuals. These are the people who must fight your wars for you. You don't want them malingering. So blow smoke. Every day, blow smoke.

Bear in mind, however, that if you treat soldiers too kindly they will rebel eventually. Treat soldiers roughly and they will follow your orders willingly.

Very often women—as subordinates—like to be treated even more roughly than male soldiers. Most people see kindness as a weakness; because of this they welcome being told what to do in direct, forceful terms. They respect strength. This is doubly true for women because their fathers were just such rough authority figures to them, and most little girls love and respect their fathers even after they have grown into women. Therefore . . .

Be prepared for betrayal from anyone on your staff, but especially from those you have the most trust in. Every betrayal must be repaid as quickly and as publicly as possible. If you should ever let a betrayal go unpunished, you are through as a leader.

Finally, if you learn that one of your soldiers or lieutenants is having domestic trouble—spouse infidelity, spouse dipsomania, kleptomania, addiction of any kind, or children experiencing juvenile catastrophes of every kind—keep a wary eye on that individual and his performance. The tree often falls very near the apple.

It is a fact that most heavy-duty managers who succeed over long periods of time seem to speak quietly, slowly, deliberately. Speaking softly forces others to listen. This ability can be acquired, and should be. But remember this too: The more you speak, the less others listen.

There will be times when you will have to be abrasive, even brutal to members of your staff. ("You—when you talk to me, shut up!") Don't worry that your people will say bad things about you because of this. They already have. But, in general, try to be pleasant and accommodating. Try to please the greatest number who work for you that you can; antagonize the fewest. Blow smoke.

Be as honest as you can with your staff. Tell them the truth about your plans—or as much of it as is necessary for them to do their jobs—or say nothing. Let them come to know you as a man of your word. (Harry Cohn, the widely hated movie czar, was nonetheless admired as a man of his word. If he said he'd destroy you, he would.) Be consistent, except occasionally—your inconsistency then used as a tactic to shake your staff out of complacency.

When you are the top man, everything you do will be seen by your staff as the mark of a genius. Or so they will say, at any rate. And most of them won't be shining you on, or even trying to. For them, an asininity becomes a profundity because you uttered it—because you are the boss. Therefore, believe no praise from a subordinate. (Your *consiglière* can be a good correcting force here.)

At meetings, have someone else float your newest ideas. Watch the reaction of the rest of your staff. Note who opposes, who supports, who links up with whom. See who responds with an open mind, whose mind is already made up, one way or the other. If you're going to walk on water, you have to know where the rocks are.

Cliques will form within your staff. There is a continuous competition for power—who gets what (bigger budget, raise or promotion, ideas adopted). Your job is to see that none of this struggle interferes with the attainment of the organization's objectives.

Information is vital to you, and the grapevine—office gossip reflecting office politicking—supplies this better than formal reports. But there is much you *don't* want to know, at least formally, so keep reports ticketed for your desk to a minimum. Unless you want to take sides on an issue between cliques, you don't have to declare yourself if you are in formal ignorance of it. Given time, the problem probably will resolve itself. In a sense, what you do is go along to get along.

The best course, then, is to meet very few internal staff problems head-on. You don't necessarily want "team play" from your staff, anyway. You want your soldiers to compete with each other for your notice and favor. (This is *not* to say that you pit them against each other.) If they know they get your notice and favor by producing, that's what you will get most often from staff rivalry: greater production.

If you have a group within your staff that is consistently producing at a high level, consistently succeeding at its tasks, don't break it up, for God's sakes. The magic of such combinations all too soon disappears of its own momentum. When you're riding a fast, fresh horse, don't get off and walk it. Ride it as long as it lasts.

Otherwise, keep shifting subordinates from task to task, group to group. If you don't, individuals will cease to think and perform well and will soak up your budget for little return.

Give troublemakers the most risky assignments and let them prove or disprove their worth. And if you're pressing hard on one part of your staff, be straight and helpful to the other parts, until it's their turn, of course.

When the situation makes it possible, don't order someone to do something. Give the task to the person who volunteers to do it. The work will be done better this way, most of the time, and you may discover yourself a promising soldier you might otherwise have overlooked.

When you do give a task to someone, give it to him only. Don't, as some management consulting firms recommend, pit two individuals against one another to accomplish the same thing. (The consultants' theory is that pitting two individuals against each other will accomplish the task

6 5   better and also reveal the better man. As Napoleon observed, however, one bad general is far better than two good generals.)

Delegate a job to one man, then. Tell him the job's objectives, then give him the authority and wherewithal to accomplish them.

Allow the widest possible discretion and choice in means, but no deviance from your timetable—without good reason—and *no* deviance from ends.

Judge on results.

Handling Staff Conflict

Let's say you hire a person who has a special skill you need. In a month or so a longer-time staff person with whom the new person must work comes to you to complain about the new person.

Evaluate in your mind the worth of the two individuals to your enterprise. If their worth is unequal, tell the complainer to try to work it out.

If time proves the two cannot coexist, get rid of the one of lesser value.

If they are of equal value, tell the complainer about the man who brought a monkey home to help him with his yardwork. The man's wife responds by telling him he's crazy. "We can't have a monkey in the house! Where will he sleep?"

"With us."

"With *us*! What about the smell?"

"He'll get used to it."

There should be no need for further discussion—but if the complainer doesn't smile, albeit ruefully, get rid of him or the trouble will continue.

Firing

In the good old days, one sentence did it: "We no longer require your services." You needed to give no reason to issue a pink slip.

Today it's a little more complicated. Terminated employees have been suing their former employers for unjust or arbitrary dismissal. Courts have been affirming the job-as-property-right concept, which means that as long as performance is good, an employee can't legally be fired.

If you want to fire someone, start documenting that individual's poor performance in writing; if and when the postfiring lawsuit comes, you'll be able to justify the termination in court. When you're preparing to get rid of someone, send out the appropriate memos about the subject's inability to handle the job, and make sure all the right people—including the targeted employee, when necessary—get copies. Some courts have warned that people can't be fired for poor performance unless they've been warned beforehand. So before you make the "soft hit," it's wise to put the victim on probation—that way he can't say he wasn't warned. At the end of the probationary period—two weeks, a month, ninety days—you usually can open wide your door and say good-bye.

A much easier, and just as effective means of getting rid of someone without having to fire him is the harassment-humiliation technique. Harsh and continuous open criticism (so that a man's colleagues can hear it) combined with humiliating orders and assignments should quickly cause a proud person to quit voluntarily.

If neither of these approaches proves effective, for one reason or another, you could always call the targeted party into your office for a private chat. What the two of you chat about is, of course, private. But if the man you want to leave returns to his desk, sits down, rubs his knees reassuringly—and fearfully—and types his resignation, you probably made your point. At that, the guy got off easy. If he had been connected to Our Thing and made any trouble about leaving, he'd have been capped, no question.

Larceny

Some of your employees are going to steal from you. It's human nature, count on it. But there are those who hold that pilfering paper clips, pens and pencils, postage stamps, and the like from the office increases job satisfaction, boosts productivity, and even helps the economy. So don't get upset if there are a few petty larcenists in your organization. But find out who they are and keep an eye on them—sometimes a small thief, emboldened by success, will try to become a big thief.

If and when you catch a big thief in your organization, make a public example of him. Nothing serves as a better deterrent to crime than the certain knowledge that swift and severe punishment will be meted out to the deviant.

Belt-Tightening

If your organization needs to tighten its belt, you and your subordinates have been lax. But if you've got to cut costs, start with yourself. It's easier for your employees to make a few sacrifices if they know the boss is doing likewise. Slash your paycheck and perks, and arrange for the accounting department to "leak" the news, so that eventually your whole company gets the word.

Begin reducing operations costs by personally examining and analyzing your entire organization. Then start ruthlessly attacking waste and redundancy. Consolidate some jobs, eliminate others. Impose strict inventory and cost controls, even down to office supplies.

Draw up a step-by-step program for becoming a leaner and meaner organization, then follow it religiously. Post that same program (with whatever deletions you deem appropriate) in a conspicuous place in the office, so that all your employees may see it and be duly inspired by the belt-tightening zeal.

Finally, make sure everyone understands the bottom line in a cost-cutting program: If you don't make it, they don't make it.

Productivity

Increased productivity does not necessarily mean working faster and putting in more hours. According to estimates, worker inefficiency runs as high as 50 percent. In other words, your employees doodle, dawdle, and daydream for thirty minutes out of every hour.

You can improve the productivity of your organization by making certain that workers have their days organized, their work planned, and objectives clearly in mind—and by a company-wide program of kicking ass.

But remember, not even a machine is 100 percent efficient. Don't expect the humans who work for you to be.

When your people are working too much overtime, either they're trying to impress you, or they can't finish their work during regular business hours. Find out which it is. You may discover that your middle-management execs are trying to advance their own fortunes by overloading their personnel. This could backfire, with everyone getting hurt, including you.

Don't encourage overtime. Tell your people that the best way to impress you is to do a great job in the time allotted for it and then go home to relax.

Rules

Your organization needs a written set of rules for its expense account policies. After that, the fewer rules, the better. Every rule is only an arbitrary border, waiting to be crossed by adventurous people. Those who would break rules may prove to be your best people.

Axioms

Rather a donkey that carries than a horse that throws.
In the fertile land of promises many have died of hunger.

The fish is killed by its open mouth.

Every button man has a capo's silk suit in his closet.

The big drum sounds good only from a distance.

You can't put a good edge on bad steel.

Occasionally suffer fools; you may learn something of value. But never argue with them.

Women resist in order to be conquered; so do some men.

Do not form your judgment of others from what you are told of them.

Patience for a moment; comfort for ten years.

With all due respect, hard likker destroys the shikker.

The eagle doesn't hunt flies.

Skate on thin ice, skate fast.

When an arrow leaves the bow, it never returns.

If you do not ask for their help, all men are good-natured.

Who pays well is served well.

All life is blind luck, even when you think you are changing it.

Money scammed is twice as sweet as money earned.

Preparation is the mother of good fortune.

Want of love or want of money lies at the bottom of all our transgressions.

No man is as fond of virtue as he is of women.

Money is welcome even if it comes in a dirty sack.

If you don't spot the mark in your first half hour at the table, you're it.

Ten countries are sooner known than some men.

A man in love—with no matter what—loses his pride and, with it, his reason. Knowledge of this helps in dealing both with subordinates and enemies.

A runaway nun always speaks ill of her convent.

A silent fool passes for a wise man; a rich thief passes for a gentleman.

A handful of luck is worth more than a truckload of wisdom.

What goes around comes around—but never in time.

In a storm, pray to God but row for shore.

Wolves lose their teeth but not their nature.

Out of fifteen who flatter, at least fourteen lie.

If a problem seemingly has no solution, look for the woman—or the man.

Deal with the facts of a bad situation as if they are worse than you know them to be. Deal with the facts of a good situation not at all.

There is always enough to go around: enough to keep, enough to reward with, enough to be stolen—as long as you first get it all.

Every remedy of a bad situation has its bad side effects. Choose the remedy with the least.

Believe the man, not the oath.

Curiosity has lost more maidenheads than love.

Many would fish but few will bring bait.

You know a soldier only when he becomes a lieutenant.

No solution satisfies everyone.

When you must cut, persuade the victim you are a surgeon.

Many words, many lies.

The capo gives part of his plan to one, part to another, the whole to none.

Simple manipulation of people—or events—is not enough. Timing is all-important.

Good medicine is always bitter.

Never worry about tomorrow. Tomorrow you might inherit a million dollars—or be run over by a truck. Or inherit a million dollars *and* be run over by a truck.

Sentiment is for suckers.

Given enough time, nothing is accomplished.

There are 2,598,960 possible five-card poker hands—but you will be dealt only one. The beauty of it is, you *don't* have to have the best hand to win.

Part III
The Rest of It

Objectives

If you don't know where you're going, you'll never get there—or anyplace else. Too few people act on this. When you leave the future to chance, it is more than likely to result in drift and disaster. Without direction, an organization falls into chaos and anarchy—and failure.

A dictatorship is the only kind of totally effective organizational governance. There are, *in fondo*, no statues of committees in public parks.

Which is to say that a dictatorship of one—you—is needed to make an organization effective. Voluntarism, cliques, many different personalities, happy social interaction among subordinates cannot. Committees cannot.

From the beginning, your personal objective was to take charge, rise to the top, to total control—that is, your objective was power. This is also the objective of the organization you manage: total control, total domination.

To reach this objective, it is up to you to assess the problems and risks and opportunities and then to devise strategies to solve the problems, minimize the risks, and seize the opportunities. You must lay out the plans for your subordinates, assign tasks: who does what, when, and where and in what sequence with what; together with deadlines.

The timetable you draw up is not a fixed one, however. It will be modified many times as your organization's resources change and with your successes and failures. It also will change as the strength of your opposition waxes and wanes and as the struggle ebbs and flows. You will never be disappointed if you expect no favors from your adversaries. You are in a war. You must plan to take the other guy down first, and do it.

Winning is not the best thing; it is the *only* thing. If it were not, no one would keep score. To win the war, you must take charge. You must set the organization's objectives, establish a chain of command, set policies, establish controls, delegate, appraise performance, adjust, and act again. In short, you must manage.

The True Nature of Business

Our Thing is about making money. Making it in any way it's possible to make it, no matter which, no matter what. So is yours, legit as it may be.

As Al Capone said back in 1926: "I am like any other man. All I do is supply a demand."

In the legit business world, cheating customers is not frowned upon so long as you are not caught at it. Nor is fleecing clients, lying, looting banks and S&Ls, defrauding widows and their children, real estate swindling, kiting stocks, loansharking, you name it. Just don't get caught.

We in Our Thing feel exactly the same. We coincide with the legit world of business in just about every other important way as well. That is, not to put too fine a point on it, we're an organization of thieves. Like the legit world's, our chief objective is to eliminate competition, to crush it. If that doesn't prove possible, we will, like execs in the legit world, agree with rivals to divide the market into separate territorial monopolies. The capitalistic price system operates through demand and supply in competitive markets. Therefore, if you want to jack up the price of your product, you strive to eliminate the competition. The hallmarks of the financial and industrial empires built by J. P. Morgan more than a century ago were a tight, efficient organization centrally controlled, together with the development of shared interests among competitors, leading to a syndicate that fixed prices and output. These are exactly the hallmarks of the Mafia empire that Johnny Torrio established in the United States back in the 1930s and that flourishes today. Syndicate crime and cartel capitalism (including that version that megaconglomerates practice) are one and the same.

All of these things you should remember about us and about the true nature of business, because knowing them will help you to put aside scruples that will hinder you in your quest for success. In any organization—at peace or at war—a complete lack of scruples confers substantial advantages.

Capitalism

As Big Al put it in 1929, "The American system of ours, call it Americanism, call it Capitalism, call it what you like, gives each and every one of us a great opportunity if we only seize it with both hands and make the most of it."

If an endorsement from Al Capone is not to your liking, here is the view of an equally prominent spokesman from the legitimate world, that of Abraham Lincoln in 1837: "These capitalists generally act harmoniously, and in concert, to fleece the public."

Fleecing the public, of course, is the true nature of business, though the thought probably could have been expressed somewhat less directly. But who would quarrel with Lincoln? *Per quanto*, the object of capitalism is to further enrich people who have money to invest (in other words, the already wealthy).

Which is why rich kids usually feel pretty good about fathers who leave them inheritance jackpots. Which is also why it's better to be rich than poor under capitalism.

In Our Thing, we love capitalism. We're nice people in other ways too, really. Just as long as you don't owe us money.

The Rich

The law, they tell us, in its majestic impartiality, forbids both the rich and the poor to sleep on park benches. In all other respects, though we are not told this (but can see it daily), the law defers to wealth. That is, money never goes to prison.

You can be rich without knowing how to be powerful (but you cannot be powerful without money). Almost all of the rich have inherited their wealth, and they believe they have their wealth as a divine right. They grow up believing deeply ("internalizing") in their inherent superiority (because God says so), and, thus, they lack almost all sympathy (and all empathy) for those with less of the world's goods than they have. They believe that poverty, for example, is also God-given, like their own wealth—and it follows for them that those with less than they have are inferior to themselves.

The idea of us lying to, cheating, or stealing from them usually does not occur to rich people. (Their money and possessions are theirs by divine right.) They therefore make interesting associates, even more interesting adversaries.

You can shear a sheep many times; you can skin him only once . . . but a rich man is a strange creature: You can both shear him and skin him again and again.

All this to alert you to the fact that if you are ever at odds with a firm headed by an individual born to wealth, you will be dealing with a strange breed of animal, one unlike your customary adversary, and you should proceed accordingly. He—the rich man—is more often than not a lollipop when crowded into a corner. All his life he has—so to say—played football as if it were a noncontact sport. *Capisci?*

In any case, remember that the main chance always will be in businesses that skin the poor, or at least not the ultra-wealthy. There are hundreds of millions of the less-than-wealthy and far more to be garnered from these millions, in total. Consider the long-term success of such companies as Firestone, Ford, General Motors, Du Pont, Union Carbide.

The Competitive Struggle

Your entire career you will be engaged in two competitive struggles, one within your organization against rivals and enemies there, the other outside the organization against its rivals and enemies. You are in the life, *compare*, and once in, you can't walk away.

In both struggles the prize is power. Not money, but power. In each struggle you seek victory in what is essentially a war. Here the words of the Prussian military theorist von Clausewitz are to the point:

"Kind-hearted people might of course think there was some ingenious way to disarm or defeat an enemy without too much bloodshed, and might imagine this is the true goal of the art of war. Pleasant as it sounds, it is a fallacy that must be exposed: War is such a dangerous business that the mistakes which come from kindness are the very worst."

The Prussian also said: "Combat is the only effective force in war; its aim is to destroy the enemy's forces as a means to a further end. . . . It follows that the destruction of the enemy's forces underlies all military actions; all plans are ultimately based on it."

Finally, take the counsel of Machiavelli on the same subject: "You must know that there are two ways to carry out a contest; the one by law, and the other by force. The first is practiced by men and the other by brutes; and as the first is often insufficient, it becomes necessary to resort to the second."

Bloody, brute behavior aimed at the total destruction of the opposition—not a price you are willing to pay for success, perhaps? Well, being kind and being a nice guy never put a carpet on anyone's office floor. And if you want to be loved, buy a beagle.

Sotto voce, here is something else you should know: It is not possible to find morality in struggles for power. Your enemies within and without the organization view you as you do them and likely regard themselves as virtuous in their attempts at mayhem upon you. In struggles for power, your judgments should be based entirely on self-interest and finding as direct and economical a route to your goal as possible. If that route is bloody and barbaric, so much the worse for those who oppose you.

To those outside the conflict, what seems right to you may seem wrong, but you can proceed only as *you* see things. This is what is meant by the phrase "You do what you have to do," with emphasis properly placed on the second *you*.

Before each battle of any war, budget your allowable losses. If your losses approach that allowable in the battle itself, cut them. The military saying is "Never reinforce failure." The poker adage is "Don't marry a losing hand." In any event, the winner is not the player who rakes in the most pots. The winner is the player who ends up with the most money.

In devising your strategies and taking action—whether force or fraud—you should strive to keep your enemy off balance. The advantage you accrue from this is chiefly in making your enemy fear you. He does not know how dangerous or effective you are, and will probe. Bluff to give him something to think about.

Let your enemy do as much of your work for you as he will. If you make it look as if he will gain by certain actions—the actions you want him to take to entrap and destroy himself—he will work for you against himself. If you have to deceive, to lie to do this, you deceive and lie. As we said, there is no morality in struggles for power.

While your intention throughout any war is to crush your opposition totally, this is not always possible; sometimes it proves out to be undesirable. But when the enemy is defeated, you must make a firm peace with him or his survivors. This is the victor's hardest job.

In making an advantageous and harmonious peace, it will be necessary to find those among the defeated who may later seek revenge and either strip them of all power or so weaken them that they can never again pose a threat to you.

Some of the defeated will—foolishly—feel grateful to you, may even thank you for bringing the contest to a conclusion. They will be abjectly submissive and even volunteer favors or further concessions beyond what you had intended to demand. Take full advantage of this weakness—before the reaction sets in.

Two things you should guard against when you have won a war: (1) the euphoria inspired by the victory; make no grandiose plans or claims while your thinking is altered by feelings inspired by triumph; and (2) the corrupting tendency of the additional power you have won. Try not to feel that much less accountable because you have that much more power. You still must answer to yourself and you must more than ever lead—that is, manage.

Negotiating

Drag negotiations on as long as you think you have a chance of gaining what you want. Your opponent may tire after a long while and become willing to make concessions. Be patient.

Don't stare your opponent in the eye during face-to-faces. *Look* him in the eye every now and then as you make your case, but don't stare. Staring, by most humans (and all dogs), is taken as an unfriendly, even menacing, act.

If pressed on a weak point, switch subjects. Use every argument you can think of when making your case—and keep repeating them. Not only will you wear your opponent down, but you never know just what argument or seeming concession will find the chink in his armor.

Play the man, not the hand; that is, whatever the strength of your opponent's position (the hand), play to your opponent's weaknesses as an individual (the man). Never give away what cards you will play, for as Machiavelli observed: "One should never show one's intentions, but endeavor to obtain one's desires anyhow. For it is enough to ask a man to give up his arms, without telling him that you intend killing him with them; after you have the arms in hand, then you can do your will with them."

Start high and stay there. This will result in a higher final offer by your opponent, including that of split-the-difference.

Give away the worthless, keep the rest. Don't sweat the small stuff.

Give your opponent many ways out. *The* fundamental rule in negotiating is that you must seem to allow your adversary at least one way out—a way to save his face—while getting him to do what you want him to do. If you don't allow him a way out—or a way that seems to be an out—it will be very difficult to get him to act, even unknowingly, in your interests.

Never renege on an outright concession—but make very few. Never threaten. As Machiavelli put it: "I hold it to be of great prudence for men to abstain from threats and insulting words towards any one, for neither the one nor the other in any way diminishes the strength of the enemy; but the one makes him more cautious, and the other increases his hatred of you, and makes him more persevering in his efforts to injure you."

Thank God for human nature; when you understand it, all negotiations—in fact, all business dealings—become much easier. People respond from greed; people respond out of fear. That's human nature.

Meetings

Memorandums

All but the most high-level meetings should be held with participants standing—and/or at the end of the day.

Assuming you are chairing the meeting, listen only as long as the speaker is saying something. This will not be long. When the speaker has talked himself out of substance, cut him off.

A meeting is over when the participants begin to repeat themselves.

Have your secretary take notes at meetings you attend and circulate to all those who have made commitments or must take action. She will know when to have you review these notes for results.

Memorandums

Ninety-nine out of every hundred memorandums that are written contain no information worth knowing. Half of the remainder will go on at least twice the length needed.

As a general rule, put nothing in writing yourself that goes beyond the general. And *never* write a truly confidential memo.

Suppliers

Instruct your subordinates to change your firm's suppliers often. To deal always with the same people for goods and services leads them to complacency and you to dependence.

An added advantage of changing suppliers with regularity is that your firm benefits from a new supplier's lowball bids to get the business. It also keeps your purchasing agent from arranging clandestine deals beneficial to himself.

Liars

▲ good liar will look you in the eye and speak in a strong, clear voice. Don't expect manifestations of "the Pinocchio syndrome" in a good liar, that is, blinking, blushing, stammering, gulping, and the like.

The best liars are sociopaths, people without a conscience. Polygraph and voice-stress analyzer tests are useless with them. Emotional and unsophisticated people, on the other hand, can "flunk" a polygraph test and still have told the truth. Anxiety and anger can cause the wrong kinds of blips on the graph and be interpreted as lies.

Screening your prospective employees by making them take the "lie detector" test is not a terribly good idea. Nor is the test effective for internal investigations.

Some people are born liars, with a pathological compulsion to subvert the truth. Given enough time, these people invariably reveal themselves. Be wary of people who talk too much; this is frequently a symptom of the compulsive liar. A poor liar will repeat certain phrases as if learned by rote—which they were.

A good liar either can be born with the gift or can develop the art after years of study, practice, and endless field work in the widest variety of circumstances. There is the well-prepared lie on one end of the spectrum and the spontaneous lie on the other—the good liar is adept at both. There are also varying degrees of truth and falsehood; the artful liar will know exactly how much fact to mix with fiction. Study the masters of deceit; statesmen and politicians, both foreign and domestic; certain lawyers, certain salesmen, some children—they offer a clue to style and content. Advertising is also worth studying, not only for its deceptive assertions but for its clever omissions as well.

Always assume an opponent is lying, the acid test as to whether he is or not being—who benefits?

Secrecy

everything leaks.

No person, no business, no government can keep a secret.

People talk—on the subway, in the elevator, at the corner bar, in the doctor's reception room, in bed, and in their sleep. The consequence of all this careless talk? The possible revelation of your company's deepest secrets—which could cost you money.

Secrets are spilled in other ways too. Sometimes a company's secrets are right out in the open in plain view for any visitor to see: on bulletin boards, at the copy machine, on scraps of paper in the wastebasket or on the floor.

You can't eliminate leaks entirely, but here are a few ways to minimize them:

Don't tell your wife, or husband, or lover, anything. One out of three married couples these days eventually get divorced. And there's no fury like the fury of an ex-spouse (or ex-lover) seeking revenge.

Don't tell your kids anything.

Don't tell anybody anything more than they need to know.

Don't have a lot of duplicate keys to critical files or safes. Keep the extras yourself, in your pocket, and at home.

Don't conduct business in public places.

Buy a good paper shredder and use it; a wastebasket is not secure.

When you have valuable company secrets to protect—

marketing plans, formulas, manufacturing techniques, mailing lists and so on—make your employees sign a confidentiality agreement promising not to reveal them to your competition. Confidentiality agreements are not entirely enforceable in some states, but they do act as a deterrent. Over the past few years, an increasing number of "trade secrets" lawsuits have been brought by employers against ex-employees who have violated an implicit trust by misappropriating confidential information. The important thing in these cases is for the employer to sue, and with much publicity, so that other potential thefts of your company secrets are deterred.

Get a safe with a changeable combination lock. Don't use your birthday, or the birthday of someone close to you, as the combination. Don't use 7-4-76, either. Change the combination frequently, but on an erratic, unpredictable schedule.

Don't give too much information to outsiders with whom you do business. Everybody likes to gossip, and even though the people you do business with may not possess critical information, smart competitors—much like paleontologists—can piece together a big secret from a few tiny fragments.

Keep a watchful eye on people who enter your place of business for service or maintenance calls or to make deliveries. This is a classic method of penetration, and your enemies will try to use it.

If your company secrets are being leaked on a regular, apparently systematic basis, and you haven't located the source, you may need a private investigative firm—or a private eye—to look into the matter. Say nothing about your suspicions; you'll give the spy or spies time to take countermeasures. Keep mum, and go directly to the best firm of private investigators you can find. They'll debug your offices, help you build an intrusion-secure environment, track down the traitors in your company (if any), and pinpoint your external enemies. It may take time and money, but you are in a war.

You may, of course, prefer to let the enemy's spies continue their espionage—and feed them false information. And one other thing: If one of your lieutenants is in charge of your own spy network, be sure that the intelligence he transmits to you does not, somehow, push toward going ahead with his own pet projects.

A Role Model

As I've said, the soldiers of the Mafia believe in honor, vengeance, and solidarity. The embodiment of these virtues in This Thing of Ours remains Johnny Torrio. Herbert Asbury, the most knowledgeable chronicler of Chicago crime, characterized him thusly: "As an organizer and administrator of underworld affairs Johnny Torrio is unsurpassed in the annals of American crime; he was probably the nearest thing to a real master mind that this country has yet produced."

Johnny Torrio was first of all, an *uomo di panza* (literally, a man of belly), a man who knows how to keep things to himself (in his guts); an *uomo segreto*, a secret, private man; but above all, an *uomo di pazienza* (patient man).

The man of patience is the man who controls. He is firm; he is constant in all things. He remains aloof from—usually at odds with—the outside society. He has no pretenses. What he has is an inner strength that gives him presence because he waits, he plans, and only at the moment of the best chance of success does he strike.

He remembers everything for possible use, learning at the expense of others. He studies their behavior, assesses what will work with them and what probably won't. While his opponents jump and twitch in impatience, he waits, gauging their weaknesses. He knows that *onore* is achieved by being worldly, shrewd, and clever and advancing one's own fortune, not by being good or trusting or acting nobly.

His whole life is one of work and self-denial, of self-reliance and self-control. He does not seek confrontations; he avoids them—unless something of paramount importance is at stake. Otherwise, he maneuvers toward his objective. He is foxy. Above all, he knows what is important, and this gives him dignity and earns him respect.

All this is his manliness too, and all of these qualities, together with intelligence, Johnny Torrio possessed to a very high degree. He learned from his few failures and mistakes in Chicago, and by the time he left the city he had acquired enough respect among his peers that when, one by one, he proposed the moves that in a comparatively short time established a U.S. National "Mafia"—the Organization—he became, de facto, the organization's *consiglière*. At seven years of age Johnny Torrio was swamping out his stepfather's blind pig in Brooklyn; half a century later—quietly—he was one of the most important and wealthy men in a nationwide criminal system—a system his ideas and energy had created, the U.S. Mafia.

You will not go far wrong should you model your own leadership style on that of Johnny Torrio. He is not as famous as the flamboyant Capone, but he was far more effective—and successful—as a leader.

Domestic Arrangements

What's marriage got to do with your business? Everything or nothing, depending on your foresight and skill. Preferably, marriage should have nothing at all to do with your business—and it's up to you and a lawyer to see that it doesn't.

Before taking vows, find yourself a lawyer who is an expert on matrimonial and divorce law. Have him draw up a prenuptial contract spelling out in detail who gets what in the event you and your spouse split up—and the odds are pretty good that you will. A small lump-sum settlement, agreed upon in advance, will keep your spouse and avaricious lawyer out of your business, your books, and your bank accounts.

When your beloved says to you: "How can you be so crassly material as to ask me to sign this agreement? Don't you love me?" you answer: "Of course I love you. But my creditors and my attorneys insist on this arrangement. Be sure to sign all four copies."

Mob marriages, of course, are never 50-50 propositions. The wife knows nothing of her husband's business. She is only vaguely, if that much, aware of his annual income, hardly knows his business associates, never expects her husband to let family matters take precedence over business necessities. Your marriage will be different, of course. You're legit. It stands to reason that you and your spouse will have a more enlightened arrangement. And yet . . .

And yet, for the sake of your career, I'd recommend that just as in Mob marriages your spouse be a person who will trust that *whatever* you do is for the best, who will (therefore) not want to be involved in decisions but will accept whatever you decide, do whatever you declare should be done—unquestioningly. It's a sorry household where the hen crows and the cock holds his peace.

Your spouse should never ask where you have been, what you have been doing, what you are thinking. A spouse should know only what you want known—and like it that way. A spouse should never be assertive, should never be angry with you. The spouse's sphere should be the home and children, nothing more.

Finito!

Axioms

Every matter has two handles.

To finish sooner, take your time.

If the only tool you have is a hammer, all problems look like nails.

Agreements are made to be broken.

There always comes a time to call in the markers.

When you compromise, you lose. When you seem to have compromised, you have taken a step toward winning.

Difficulties show what men are.

Preparation is the mother of good fortune, daring is the father.

The wife of a careless man is almost a widow.

Long after other sins are old, avarice remains young.

If you are the anvil, be patient; if you are the hammer, strike.

If your plans prosper, everyone will be your friend; if your plans fail—only then will you find your true friends.

Ill luck comes in pairs—and then more.

Never expect logic and reason to govern human affairs.

Fortune smiles and then betrays.

The wrong choice usually seems the more reasonable.

When events are at their worst, they can only get better.

Fortune is on the side of the strong.

When you have a lock, give your opponent an out.

For peace, be ready for war.

Never make an enemy you don't have to.

Don't teach your soldiers all your cunning, or you may fall victim to yourself.

Better that your enemies overestimate your stupidity than your shrewdness.

To deceive an enemy, pretend you fear him.

A louse in the cabbage is better than no meat at all.

The future is purchased with the present.

After a war, many heroes present themselves.

Misfortunes always come in by the door that has been left open for them.

After a victory, sharpen your knife.

If you are never in the street, you cannot know it.

If the others fold every time you bet a good hand, you are playing to their eyes.

Strike first and you will strike last.

No crisis is as bad as it can be imagined.

Let sleeping dogs lie unless you have a lion on your leash.

No one dies twice.

Victories are always temporary; so are defeats.

The best theories very often make the worst practice.

Silence makes no mistakes.

Let your adversary talk. When he has finished, let him talk some more.

Men may be bribed in a variety of coin.

Treat a stranger as a friend; trust him as you would a stranger.

Calm waters may conceal sharks.

There is no such thing as a cheap politician.

To live by another's will is misery to a few, necessary to many, happiness to most. Act on this.

Anger is the wind that blows out the candle of the mind.

Enough is not a feast—it is only enough.

In the sea, all men are brothers—but those with a lifebuoy may not be willing to share it.

Only a fool turns back at the goal.

Many a difference can be resolved between the sheets.

Never tie up a dog with the gut of a pig.

Fear is often concealed by daring.

An enemy is most dangerous when he appears defeated.

Deceive the rich, but don't insult them.

When you hunt, let the game come to you.

The old age of an eagle is like its youth: full of peril.

. . . And a man's cradle stands in his grave.

Wherever you go, there you are. *Basta.*